First Facts™

Animal Behavior

Animals Sleeping

by Wendy Perkins

Capstone
press
Mankato, Minnesota

First Facts is published by Capstone Press
151 Good Counsel Drive, P.O. Box 669, Mankato, Minnesota 56002
http://www.capstonepress.com

Library of Congress Cataloging-in-Publication Data
Perkins, Wendy.
    Animals sleeping / by Wendy Perkins.
    p. cm.—(First facts. Animal behavior)
    Summary: Simple text explains the varied ways in which such animals as flamingos, ball
pythons, dolphins, and horses sleep.
    Includes bibliographical references and index.
    ISBN 0-7368-2511-8 (hardcover)
    1. Sleep behavior in animals—Juvenile literature. [1. Animals—Sleep behavior. 2. Animals
Habits and behavior.] I. Title. II. Series.
QL755.3.P47 2004
591.5'19—dc22   2003015214

Editorial Credits
Erika L. Shores, editor; Jennifer Bergstrom, series designer; Wanda Winch, photo researcher;
    Eric Kudalis, product planning editor

Photo Credits
Ann & Rob Simpson, 5, 13
Bruce Coleman Inc./Bill Wood, 15; Colla V&W, 10–11; Jeff Foott, 19; Joe McDonald, 9, 14;
    Pat & Rae Hagan, 8
Corbis/Jim Zuckerman, cover
Creatas, 6–7
Minden Pictures/John Eastcott/Yva Momatiuk, 16–17; Michael and Patricia Fogden, 20

**First Facts thanks Bernd Heinrich, Ph.D., Department of Biology, University of
Vermont in Burlington, Vermont, for reviewing this book.**

1 2 3 4 5 6 09 08 07 06 05 04

Table of Contents

A Sleeping Flamingo

A flamingo steps slowly through a **marsh** at sunset. It stops between two other flamingos. The bird lifts up one leg against its body. It tucks its beak under a wing. The wing's feathers cover the leg and beak. The flamingo closes its eyes. It sleeps safely with its **flock**.

Safe Sleeping

An animal becomes still when it sleeps. A sleeping animal may not hear quiet sounds. Some sleeping animals cannot tell when danger is near. **Predators** may attack sleeping animals. Many animals have ways to sleep safely.

Fun Fact:
A harp seal pup sleeps hidden under snow. The pup's white fur makes it hard for a predator to spot it in the snow.

Hide and Sleep

Some animals hide when they sleep. Rabbits sleep in **burrows**. Rabbits hide in these underground homes to stay safe from predators.

A ball python sleeps coiled in a ball. The python looks like the leaves around it. Other animals may not see the snake. It hides while out in the open.

Fun Fact:
Snakes do not have eyelids. They sleep with their eyes open.

Animals That Rest

Some animals sleep a little bit at a time. Dolphins rest near the top of the ocean. Dolphins keep one eye open while they sleep. Part of the dolphin's brain knows what is happening around it.

Fun Fact:
Dolphins have to remember to breathe. A dolphin might not breathe if it goes into a deep sleep.

Safe in a Group

Animals in a group help each other stay safe. Pillbugs crowd together under dead leaves to rest. Pillbugs are safer in a group because liquid inside a pillbug tastes bad to predators. A predator that eats one pillbug will leave the rest alone.

Fun Fact:
Pillbugs do not breathe air. They have gills that take oxygen from moisture.

13

Weird Sleepers

Some animals do amazing things to stay safe while they rest. Bats sleep hanging from cave ceilings. Predators cannot reach them.

A parrotfish covers itself with **mucus** before it sleeps. The thick film looks like a plastic bag. This slimy **sac** keeps predators from smelling the parrotfish.

Standing Sleepers

Many animals do not lie down to sleep. Horses usually sleep standing up.

Not every horse in a **herd** sleeps at the same time. Some horses only nap. They can spot danger and warn the other horses.

Fun Fact:
A horse that feels safe will lay down to sleep.

Animals Sleeping

All living things need time to rest. Rabbits sleep safely in burrows. Bats sleep hanging upside down. Horses usually sleep standing up. How does a squirrel sleep?

Amazing But True!

Sloths sleep for almost 20 hours a day. These rain forest animals hang upside down in trees. They even sleep upside down. Sloths move very slowly when they are awake. It looks as if they are hardly moving at all.

Hands On: Your Heartbeat

When living creatures sleep, their heartbeats slow down. You can see how this happens to your own body by comparing your heartbeat at night and in the morning.

What You Need

clock or watch with a second hand
paper
pencil

What You Do

1. At bedtime, count your heartbeats. Place your index and middle fingers of one hand on your neck just below your jaw. Count how many times your heart beats in six seconds.
2. Write the number of heartbeats on a piece of paper. Add a zero to the end of the number. This new number shows how many times your heart beats each minute.
3. Write the word "evening" beside the number.
4. In the morning, before you get out of bed, repeat steps 1-2. Write the word "morning" beside this number.
5. Keep track of your evening and morning heartbeats for a week.

When does your heart beat the fastest? When does your heart beat the slowest?

Glossary

burrow (BUR-oh)—a tunnel or hole in the ground made or used by an animal

flock (FLAHK)—a group of animals of one kind that live, travel, or eat together

herd (HURD)—a large group of animals that live together

marsh (MARSH)—an area of wet, low land where grasses grow

mucus (MYOO-kuhss)—a slimy, thick fluid

predator (PRED-uh-tur)—an animal that hunts other animals for food

sac (SAK)—a part of a plant or animal that is shaped like a pocket or bag

Read More

Giles, Bridget. *Parrotfish.* Nature's Children. Danbury, Conn.: Grolier, 2001.

Kajikawa, Kimiko. *Sweet Dreams: How Animals Sleep.* New York: Henry Holt, 1999.

Swanson, Diane. *Animals Can Be So Sleepy.* Vancouver: Greystone Books, 2001.

Internet Sites

FactHound offers a safe, fun way to find Internet sites related to this book. All of the sites on FactHound have been researched by our staff.

Here's how:
1. Visit *www.facthound.com*
2. Type in this special code **0736825118** for age-appropriate sites. Or enter a search word related to this book for a more general search.
3. Click on the Fetch It button.

FactHound will fetch the best sites for you!

Index